Over 50

Secret Codes

Emily Bone

Illustrated by
Samantha Meredith

HORSES
IGLOO
DATE
DRINK
EAGLE
NATION
MIRROR

EVENT
SEAT
SWORD
ACCENT
GROUP
EIGHT
SOUP

No. 1 Agency

Important code

Agent Smith is working for the No. 1 Agency, an undercover organization dedicated to fighting crime and solving mysteries. He has been given the information on the right, and coded instructions for his mission below. Can you help him by decoding the symbols?

◎++⊓ ⊤/+<⊓ ↓ ⊤⊓
⊓人+ ↑∅✳ ◎⊤□⇐+⊓
⊓↑ ⇒‖☆⇐ 刀⇒ ()↑刀□
✳‖△/刀‖△+
△人+ !‖∅∅ 人⊤?+ ⊤
□+✳ □↑△+

TOP SECRET

$< \uparrow \Rightarrow \bigcirc \square \triangle \sqcap \nearrow ?\,!$

$\diamondsuit$

$\circledcirc$

$\oslash$

$()$

$\Leftarrow$

Φ

$=$

$\gg$

$\|$

$\ll$

λ

$/$

The symbol for A is shown in the red box on the opposite page. Letters B to Z, then digits 0 to 9, follow around the border of this page in the direction indicated by the box's arrow.

$\not\equiv$

$\Uparrow$

$+ \ast \,\,\bigstar\,\, \cap \top\, \downarrow\,\nabla\, \infty\, 8\, \not\leq$

Detective disguise

ACE

♠

AGENCY

:esiugsid fo retsam a eb ot woH

1) .noitnetta yrassecennu tcartta ton oD
.lamron skool taht yaw a ni tca syawlA

2) .uoy dnuora elpoep eht dna sgnidnuorrus
ruoy htiw ni dnelb uoy ekam taht sehtolc raeW

3) .ecaf ruoy edih ylkciuq nac uoy taht os
feihcrekdnah egral ro repapswen a yrraC

4) .nac uoy revenehw, seert ekil, sgniht
dniheb ediH

5) .esiugsid ruoy egnahc ylkciuq, dettops
neeb evah uoy kniht uoy fI

Katy Kode has just joined a private detective firm called the Ace Agency. On her first day, she receives a file giving guidelines on how to be a detective, including information on how to follow someone without being spotted. The only problem is that the guidelines are in code...

Look at the document on the left and write down the five ways that detectives can avoid being noticed when on a mission.

1.

2.

3.

4.

5.

Testing tourist guide

Detective Dot has been monitoring the sunny island of Konos as there is a suspected criminal gang, the Bad Brothers, at work there. Flicking through a tourist guide, the detective has noticed something strange – someone has made marks on one of the pages. Could it be some kind of secret code? See if you can help Detective Dot by finding the hidden message.

Welcome to Konos. We hope you enjoy your stay here. You must visit the ancient ruins situated outside the old town. Dating back to 1400 BC, the ruins were once a bustling city, home to the famous Konos people. The Konos were ahead of their time, inventing many new tools.

They also had a thriving craft industry, trading their goods with nearby villages at weekly markets. The city's buildings were beautifully decorated with impressive carvings and they built grand temples...

Reverse code

In a reverse code, a message is written out, then split into groups of different numbers of letters. So 'Meet you at the station at six' could be written:

MEET YO UAT THE ST AT IONA TSIX

Then, each group is written back-to-front:

TEEM OY TAU EHT TS TA ANOI XIST

The letter below has been written using reverse code. Can you crack it?

RAED TRA RUH,
RGNOC UTA AL NOIT NOS UOY
ER CS EPA. EVAHI AEH DR
NUOY EE LEHD ACOTP HCT EHT
EP LPO OHWE DIK EPPAN UOYD.
LIWI LL EVAE BA WOR APN KC
OEGA HTN APE KR CNEB ENH
TRA EH BRAM EL TATS EU. DEW
DSEN YA. ENIN MP.
GIS DEN FR.

Ancient Egyptian mystery code

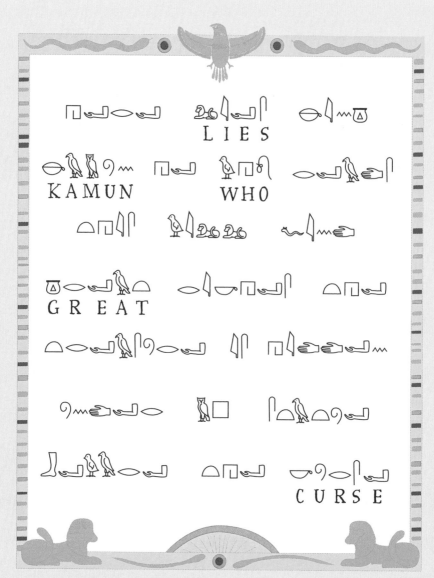

LIES

KAMUN   WHO

GREAT

CURSE

Professor Sands is an expert on Ancient Egypt. He has recently been studying objects found in the tomb of an Egyptian king and has discovered a stone slab with some ancient symbols carved into it. He has been able to decipher some of the symbols, but he needs help to decode the rest of them and read the message.

Look at the symbols on the left. Can you help the professor decode the message? Write the message under the symbols.

Next, see if you can decode this message, also found in the king's tomb:

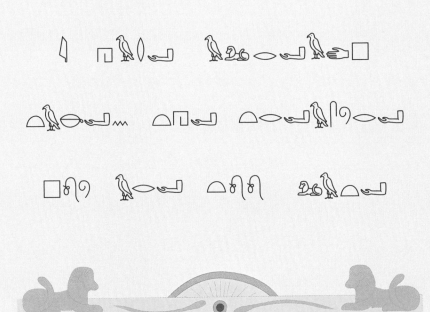

Arctic adventure

Agent A is an experienced spy working for the International Intelligence Service. For her next mission, she has been told to follow Frosty Frank, a known enemy agent. Frank has a base near the North Pole, where temperatures reach far below freezing and there are constant snowstorms. Agent A has never been to the Arctic before, so her boss has given her a document listing useful equipment – but it's written in code. Can you help Agent A write down what she needs for her trip?

IssentiaE crctiA tquipmene:

1. hrasc -froop, rotom-dowerep enowmobils
2. trosf-tesistanr oadir
3. wnos-nisiov soggleg
4. rolap reab tepellenr
5. eortablp eicrowavm

1

A	H
O	V

2

B	I
P	W

3

C	J
Q	X

4

D	K
R	Y

5

E	L
S	Z

6

F	M
T

7

G	N
U

...this code, you have to use the crosses on the left.

...start with, find the letter you want to put into code.

... example, if you wanted to put the letter 'D' into

...oss code, you would find it here in cross no. 4: $\dfrac{D\,|\,K}{R\,|\,Y}$

...ite ___ to show where the letter appears in the

...oss, and 4 to show which cross the letter appears

..., like this: 4⌋

...e if you can understand these messages written in

...oss code:

1. 1⌋6 2⌋7 5⌋1   5⌋7 5⌋6 ⌈4   1⌋ 7⌋ 5⌋7 6⌋ 5⌉
    6⌉ 1⌋6 1⌉ 4⌉ 4⌉ 1⌉2   ⌊7 ⌊2 7⌋⌊1 6⌉

2. 1⌋ 7⌋ 5⌋7 6⌉   ⌈4 5⌋ 4⌋   7⌋ 1⌉
    7⌉7 4⌋ 5⌉ 4⌉ 3⌋ ⌈7⌉⌈1 5⌋ 4⌉

Mystery at the deserted house

Secret Agent Sami has intercepted a coded message that could lead to the capture of a criminal gang. Look at the message below. Can you guess what some of the words are and help Agent Sami by finding out which letter each number stands for? Write the decoded words under each line, and begin filling in the table.

W1   M9S7   M117   87   N5N1

697S5D1   7H1   6LD   H69S1.

5   H8V1   7H1   M6N1Y.

1	E
5	
6	
7	
8	
9	
15	
18	
20	
24	

Now use these numbers to decode extra information about the case and complete the table. (// = end of word)

7 H 1 // G 6 L 15 // F 18 6 M // 7 H 1 //

L 8 S 7 // J 6 20 // 5 S // H 5 15 15 1 24 //

9 24 15 1 18 // 7 H 1 // S 7 8 5 18 S //.

Shopping list code

Secret messages can be hidden in lots of everyday things such as books, newspapers and even shopping lists. See if you can find the message hidden in the coded shopping list below. Clue: look carefully at the number next to each item — it might help you to crack the code.

Shopping List

1 melon
7 potatoes
6 oranges
1 tomato
1 mango
3 cheeses
2 bananas
1 tart
6 apples
6 chicken legs
1 vase
5 grapefruits
5 lemons

Now, can you decode the secret message
hidden in this shopping list, too?

Shopping List

1 chocolate bar
5 carrots
1 dog toy
3 cream cakes
1 notepad
5 pizzas
1 meringue
2 red apples
1 bottled water
2 calculators
1 nectarine
6 red snappers
3 pencils
2 lamb cutlets

Decoy code

THIS WAY

NO, THIS WAY

In this code, a decoy word or phrase is mixed in with the message. The message is written out with a space between each letter, so 'Agent Q good to go' looks like:

A G E N T Q G O O D T O G O

A decoy phrase such as CODE RED is then written in the spaces and repeated as many times as necessary:

ACGOEDNETRQEGDOCOODDTEORGEO

To make the coded message harder to decipher, it is split into groups:

ACG OED NET RQE GDO COO DDT EOR GEO

See if you can find out the meaning and decoy word or phrase in these coded messages. Write out the meaning above the message and the decoy below it.

1. LFEO AOVT EPAR FIAN LTSF EOTO RTAP IRL

2. SCPH EAAN KGWE IVTO HIAC NEAC CHCA ENNG TE

3. GCIOVN EFAUDS IEFCFO ENRFEU NSTENC AOMNE

Caesar's code

Julius Caesar was a Roman general who used this substitution code to send secret messages during battles. Using a scroll like the one on the right, 'A' was written under a chosen 'key' letter. Then, the rest of the alphabet was written under the letters from there (continuing from the scroll's 'A' after the end of the scroll's alphabet was reached). A message was **coded** by finding each letter in the top row and replacing it with the letter written below.

See if you can work backwards to **decode** the two messages below, using a different set of the scroll's lines for each one. The first word in each message has already been translated. Write in the code letter for 'A' and use it as your starting point.

1. **MXQJ WQCU TE IUSHUJ QWUDJI FBQO?**

   WHAT

   Y-IFO!

2. **PATM WH RHN VHHD YHK T LXVKXM TZXGM?**

   WHAT

   LIR-ZAXMMB!

ABCDEF

— — — — — —

— — — — — —

GHIJKLM

— — — — — — —

— — — — — — —

NOPQRST

— — — — — — —

— — — — — — —

UVWXYZ

— — — — — — —

— — — — — — —

Spiral code

This spiral code starts simply enough, but is tough to crack. A message is written out in lines of four. Any extra spaces on the last line are filled with an 'X'.

```
I N V I
S I B L
E W R I
T I N G
```

In order to code the message, a spiral is drawn over the letters, starting in the top left corner and going into the middle of the letters, like this.

```
I N V I
S I B L
E W R I
T I N G
```

The message is then written out, following the spiral:

INVILIGNITESIBRW

See if you can decipher the codes below by writing them out in spirals:

1. POISDRALLEUONEBM

2. SPYVOGSELGNISIOG

3. MAGNILXSSANIFYGG

Dummy code no. 1

In this devious code, a message is broken up into groups that are two, four or six letters long. A random dummy letter is then put in the middle of each group. For example, 'Leave messages in false code' can be divided into groups of four:

LEAV EMES SAGE SINF ALSE CODE

Then, dummy letters are added:

LEOAV EMYES SAGGE SIDNF ALPSE COIDE

Can you decode the messages below?

1. ALMLT HETMO NEXYF OULND LAFST

NIPGH TIYSF AKVER EPBOR TTOOQ.

2. THPER EAMLM ONNEY WAFSS ENZTO

VETRS EABSY ESKTE RDFAY.

3. MXO NZI TKO RSA LML KHN OMW NQS

PTY GGA NOG SLI NPL OBC ADL ASR EFA.

Now, using the instructions on the left, put the following messages into dummy code. There is more than one way of coding each message...

4. WE HAVE NOTICED TRICKY TREVOR AND SLY SAM ACTING SUSPICIOUSLY.

5. WATCH THESE ENEMY SPIES VERY CLOSELY THEY MAY LEAD US TO THE REAL MONEY.

6. COME QUICK AND SEND BACK UP WE KNOW THE LOCATION OF THE REAL MONEY AND HAVE CAUGHT THE THIEVES.

Trio code

The trio code is a simple code. A message is written out in groups of three, like this:

CON TAC TSP YMA STE RHQ

Each group of three is then mixed up so that the first letter in each group is moved into the middle:

OCN ATC STP MYA TSE HRQ

See if you can decode these messages:

1. AWT HCF ROA EGN 1T9.

2. AWI FTO FRU TRH REI SNT URC ITO SNA EGN STM TIH.

3. OTS GIN LAF ROH LEP ARI ESY UOR IRG THH NAD.

4. OCD REE ADG NET EGT UOT ONW!

5. WATCH FOR WOMAN CARRYING RED BAG.

6. AGENT YELLOW YOU ARE BEING FOLLOWED.

7. RETURN TO AGENCY HEAD OFFICE.

8. MEETING IS AT SEVEN. DO NOT BE LATE.

Number jumble

14 21 13 2 5 18 10 21 13 2 12 5

The line above looks like a random jumble of numbers,
but it's actually a code where numbers stand for letters.
Above, 1=A, 2=B and so on in a sequence until 26=Z. If
you decode the message it says 'number jumble'.

This code can have lots of variations with different
numbers standing for different letters, for example 2=A,
4=B, and so on. See if you can decode the message below by
working out which letters the numbers stand for and
filling in the table. The first part of the message has been
decoded to help you.

A	B	C	D	E	F	G	H	I	J	K	L	M
N	O	P	Q	R	S	T	U	V	W	X	Y	Z

1. 3 15 14 20 1 3 20 8 17 9
   C O N T A C T H

13 13 5 4 9 1 20 5 12 25.

Read the instructions on the left first, then use this
table to help you decode the messages below as well.

A	B	C	D	E	F	G	H	I	J	K	L	M

N	O	P	Q	R	S	T	U	V	W	X	Y	Z

2. 46   2   36   28   18   28   14   50   30   42
   W   A   R   N   I   N   G   Y

2   36   10   4   10   18   28   14   12   30   24

24   30   46   10   8.

3. 45   1   39   5   15   37   25   17   39   15   5
   W   A   T   C   H   S   M

23   29   37   9   23   49   37   15   9   17   37

1   37   31   49.

Mangara deco

MANGARA DECO
ANAGRAM CODE

Can you understand the title on the left? It should read 'anagram code', but the letters of each word have been jumbled up.

Messages turned into anagrams have had the order of the letters in each word scrambled. The messages are even harder to decipher when the order of the words is mixed up too.

Read the messages below and find out what each one says.

1. KAFE DAN BREAD A GWI.

2. NDA THA KARD SLASGES.

3. PLMI A KLAW WHIT.

4. CLAKB YEE NAD ILNGS.

Sandwich code

The sandwich code is a quick and easy way of disguising secret messages. The first half of a message is written out, leaving a gap between each letter. So, 'Meet you on the bank by the river' is written:

M E E T Y O U O N T H E B

The second half of the message is written in the gaps:

MAENEKTBYYOTUHOENRTIHVEEBR

The coded message is then divided into groups to make it harder to decipher:

MA EN EK TB YY OT UH OE NR TI HV EE BR

See if you can work out the sandwiched messages below:

1. TOHN EEWD ADTO ENRO ITSD PROI INSK.

2. MBEY ETTH IENH POAT RDKO WGIS LTLA BNED.

3. IS NI SN TL RO UC CK TE IR O1 N4.

Read the instructions on the left, then put the following messages into the sandwich code. There is more than one way of coding each message...

4. THE SUSPECT HAS COFFEE AT THE

RESTAURANT ON EAST STREET EVERY DAY.

5. WATCH HIM CLOSELY AND WRITE DOWN

WHAT TIME HE LEAVES THE RESTAURANT.

6. REPORT BACK TO HQ ON THURSDAY

USING THE SANDWICH CODE.

Suspected enemy agent

there
ange
re in
y of
fter
ne
an
nt
n

Have you noticed anything suspicious?

At the Daily Tribune, we were shocked to discover that an enemy agent might be hiding out among us. We have eyewitness reports that Dr. White, of Furness Drive, was seen meeting with a suspicious-looking gentleman on Monday. A day later he was spotted again with the same man. This time, they exchanged packages in a dark alleyway and parted quickly. Nobody has been able to provide a full description of the other gentleman. Can you help? Please write to us if you have any information.

s
V
g
A
wo

Agent M is working for the government's code-breaking department. It's his job to examine documents that might be hiding secret messages.

Sifting through today's paper, Agent M notices an interesting article about a suspected enemy agent. Reading the article, he realizes there is something strange about the words. Could it be hiding something?

Look at the article on the left and help Agent M discover the hidden message.

Top Secret

A B C D E F G H I J K L M N O P Q R S T U V W X Y Z

Carta Tarkos

Special Agent Zac is on a top-secret mission in the ancient jungles of Carta Tarkos. He has been working undercover for several weeks, when he is sent the innocent-looking postcard on the right. The postcard shows 'places of interest' in the area. However, he thinks that the red dots might be concealing a secret message giving him important instructions for his mission. Can you help Zac work out what the message says?

Look for a device concealed along the edge of an earlier page in this book. Use it to decode the message on the map. Clue: turn the book so the postcard is at the top, then start at the top of the map and work down...

● Places of interest

Hidden word code

SATSUMAS
HELP
ARRIVE
DOWN
OVER
WAITRESS

At first sight, the list on the left looks like random words. Now, look at the first letter of each word and see what they spell. They are hiding the word 'SHADOW'.

See if you can find the hidden messages in these groups of words:

1. FINISH   MEAT
   OLIVE   ACTING
   LANE   NIBBLE
   LABEL   INDIA
   OWL   NIGHT
   WOULD   HOOP
   WEATHER   ANIMAL
   OTHER   TANGO

2. KEEP   STORIES
   YOU   LOG
   OUT   EMU
   TOO   SKI
   MEAN   MISS
   CARD   COFFEE
   SAFARI

1.

2.

Read the instructions on the left, then try disguising
the secret messages below using the hidden word code.
There is more than one way of coding the messages...

PASSWORD IS FROG

Make each of the words you use to hide the
message the name of a type of food.

SPY CAMERA

Try making each word the name of an animal.

Looping lines code

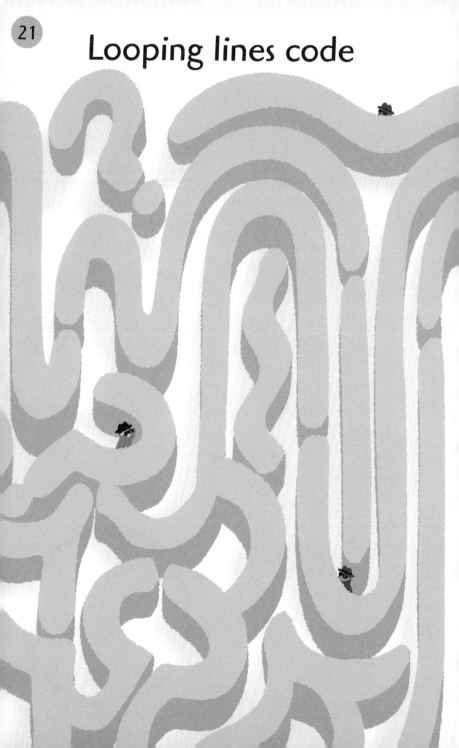

Messages coded using the looping lines code look hard to crack unless you know how they've been written.

First, a message is written out in lines of four or five. If the last line is a little short, any extra spaces are filled with an 'X'.

B E C A
R E F U
L A G E
N T Y X

To code the message, a looping line is drawn down the first column of letters, then up the next column, and so on.

B E C A
R E F U
L A G E
N T Y X

The letters are written out in that order:

BRLN TAEE CFGY XEUA.

See if you can decode the secret messages below:

1. **TLBV EYEU RFRR XITN**

2. **MAOO ASTE ECSD SRRT**

3. **DTIIO ONNII ROCEM 3TANE CSBR6**

Keyword code

A B C D E F

‒ ‒ ‒ ‒ ‒ ‒

‒ ‒ ‒ ‒ ‒ ‒

‒ ‒ ‒ ‒ ‒ ‒

G H I J K L M

‒ ‒ ‒ ‒ ‒ ‒ ‒

‒ ‒ ‒ ‒ ‒ ‒ ‒

‒ ‒ ‒ ‒ ‒ ‒ ‒

N O P Q R S T

‒ ‒ ‒ ‒ ‒ ‒ ‒

‒ ‒ ‒ ‒ ‒ ‒ ‒

‒ ‒ ‒ ‒ ‒ ‒ ‒

U V W X Y Z

‒ ‒ ‒ ‒ ‒ ‒

‒ ‒ ‒ ‒ ‒ ‒

‒ ‒ ‒ ‒ ‒ ‒

This code works by using a keyword that doesn't have any repeated letters in it. Write the keyword directly below the start of the alphabet on the left, then add the rest of the alphabet, leaving out the letters used in the keyword. So, if the keyword 'CAREFUL' was used, it would look like this:

ABCDEFGHIJ...
CAREFULBDG...

A message is coded by finding each letter in the top row and replacing it with the letter below.

Use the keyword 'CAREFUL' to crack the first message below. Each message will reveal a new keyword to use in the next message. Can you crack them all?

1. SBF HFYWMPE UMP JFQQCLF SWM DQ EFRMYQ

2. RBY HYXVLPO SLP JYQQDAY RBPYY FQ KFABR

3. WTJJ HMLT! YMU CNVT GQNGFTH NJJ SCT GMHTR!

Tricky train journey

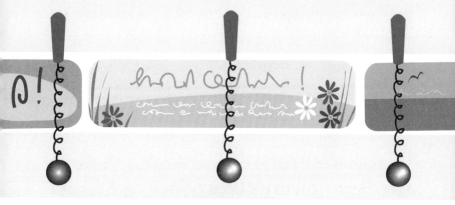

Frankie, the undercover spy, is sitting on a train and sees that there are some scratches on the window. On closer inspection, she notices that the scratches are actually symbols. Is it a coded message? Look at the symbols on the left and help her to decode the message. Read the instructions for code 7 for clues.

Frankie gets off the train and looks around for more clues. Reading a poster, she thinks she can spy a secret message. Can you help her work out what it says? (Hint: look at code 20 in this book.)

Hello, Enter Life's Play Time. Enjoy Lovely Luxury. Have Quality And Good Experiences. Nearly Ten Years In Sun. Maybe? It's Super! Say It Now. Goodness.

Sly Sam's diary

October 15th

Only four days to go until the big day.
This is the biggest job we've
attempted so far. I'm so excited!
Although I am worried about getting
the timing right. If we are a minute
late it will go all wrong... The City
Museum is supposed to be guarded at
all times. But one guard always leaves
early, at eight thirty pm. The next
guard doesn't start his shift until eight
forty. So we'll have ten minutes to
disable the alarm system, and take the
Egyptian jewels without being seen. I
hope nothing goes wrong. These jewels
are worth millions...

Sly Sam is the leader of one of the country's most wanted criminal gangs, The Sticky Fingers, who specialize in stealing priceless jewels from museums.

So far, the police have not been able to catch them because all the gang members communicate with each other in secret code.

During a recent raid, Detective Jones came across Sly Sam's diary. He found he could not understand the coded language inside.

Look at the diary page on the left, and help Detective Jones by writing down the location, date and time of the gang's next crime and what they plan to steal.

LOCATION:

DATE:

TIME:

ITEM:

Spy facts

CLASSIFIED

IMPORTANT AGENCY
INFORMATION

AGENT W

AGENT X

See if you can understand the 'spy facts' below that have been disguised using a secret code. To start with, you will have to discover which code has been used. (Hint: look at code 4 to help you.)

1. EHT OQH NAF PSY GAY CNE SIY LAC DEL CNU EL.

2. DA UO LB AE EG TN SI SA YP HT TA OW KR FS RO WT CO UO TN IR SE TA HT SE MA TE EMI.

3. AEDA ORDD ASIP RCES LPTE WECA EREH EIPS AELS APEV GAKC ROSE SSEM SEGA EBOT KCIP PUDE.

Puzzling numbers

1	2	3	4	5	
A	B	C	D	E	1
F	G	H	I	J	2
K	L	M	N	O	3
P	Q	R	S	T	4
U	V	W	X	YZ	5

To decode a message, find each letter in the grid on the
left. For each letter, look at the number at the top of
the column and at the end of the row. For example, the
letter 'L' would be coded as 23.

See if you can understand these coded messages:

1. 54 32 51 14 11 44 44 35 53 34

41 42 44 34 51 41 12 53 45.

2. 12 53 23 23 53 35 11 22 51 43

54 21 23 11 31 13 43 53 35.

3. 14 11 31 13 11 22 51 11 54 41

51 11 41 41 34 53 14.

Cryptic crossword

Uncle Ali is a retired secret agent who is an expert in codes and riddles.

His nephew, James, has come to visit. James knocks at the front door but no one answers. He tries to open it but finds it locked. Looking for another way in, he discovers that the back door is open. There is still no sign of anyone in the house...

The only thing left out on the kitchen table is the crossword puzzle, with some letters missing. His uncle never fails to complete it, so James begins to wonder whether the missing letters might spell out a secret message.

Can you guess what some of the unfinished words are, and help James work out what the hidden message says? Remember, the letters you add have to make words for **all** the answers they are part of, and no names of people or places are allowed.

Semaphore code

A B C D E F G

H I J K L M N

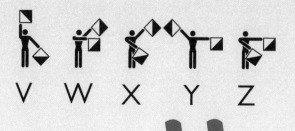

O P Q R S T U

V W X Y Z

Before the invention of radio, sailors needed a quick and easy way of sending messages to people on nearby land — especially when there was an emergency. They used a code called semaphore where flags held in different positions stood for letters and numbers. It is still used on ships today when there is no access to radio.

See if you can understand these different semaphore messages using the key on the left.

1.

2.

3.

Agent Mia's message

Mia is an undercover agent who has infiltrated a criminal gang. She has found a message written by one of the gang members. At first glance, the message looks like gibberish but then she sees that it's in code. Read the message and help Agent Mia by noting down important information.

To Big Bad Bob,

Everything is in place for midnight tonight.
I have delivered the package to Sandy the Snitch.
She will signal to me when Fingers McCoy leaves
the building. The boys will drive up in the red car
and snatch Fingers before he suspects a thing.

Dangerous Dave

Time:

Intended target:

Names of criminals involved:

Morse code

A = .−   L = .−..   V = ...−

B = −...   M = −−   W = .−−

C = −.−.   N = −.   X = −..−

D = −..   O = −−−   Y = −.−−

E = .   P = .−−.   Z = −−..

F = ..−.   Q = −−.−   End of letter = /

G = −−.   R = .−.   End of word = //

H = ...   S = ...

I = ..   T = −

J = .−−−   U = ..−

K = −.−

Telegraph key

Before the invention of phones and text messages, Morse code was a quick way to send messages. Each letter of the alphabet was written as a number of long 'dashes' (-) and short 'dots' (.). The code was sent by an operator who tapped each letter as long and short sounds with a telegraph key. The taps were changed into electrical signals that were transmitted through telegraph wires to a receiver, then decoded back into letters.

Use the patterns of dashes and dots on the left to decode the message below:

--/ · / · /-//--/ · // ·· /--//- / ···· / · // ··-/

··· /··-/·-/·-··//-··· /·-··/··-/-·--/· //··//····/

··-/····/· //-/····/·//--/---/-·/·/-·--//

-··/---//-·/---/-//-··/·//··-·/·/-/·//

Crime code conundrum

Detective Dan works for a top-secret organization that specializes in cracking coded messages. He has recently intercepted a series of messages between Bad Bruno and Terrible Tyson, who work for one of the most feared criminal gangs in the country.

Can you help Detective Dan understand what Bruno and Tyson are saying to each other?

Airport mix-up

Rob Riddle has just come back from visiting friends. He picked up his suitcase from the luggage carousel at the airport and returned home only to find that he's got the wrong case. He tries to read the address label, but it looks as if it's in code. Can you help Rob find out whose suitcase he has picked up? (Hint: look at code 10 for clues.)

MARGWEINLTLXIAS GLEONNTDXOAN

....

GEENNGTLXAANGD

....

Rob opens the case to find out more, but it's empty except for a piece of paper with numbers all over it. Using code 26, can you help Rob decode the message?

14 23 51 11 44 51 32 51 23 14. 42 11 33 42 43

54 32 51 32 11 43 41 44 53 12 51 43 51 33 55

44 14 42 51 44. 54 51 23 23 32 24.

Margaret's mysterious mail

Abi is spending the summer with her Aunt Margaret. Margaret is teaching Abi all kinds of things, such as how to disguise herself in a crowd and how to write in code. Abi doesn't know much about her aunt, apart from the fact that she works 'for the government' and is always going on trips to faraway places.

Abi gets up one morning to discover that her aunt has disappeared. After searching the house for clues, she finds a strange letter that doesn't make any sense at all. There's no one called Anna in Abi's family! She starts to think the marks on the page might be a code her aunt has taught her in which a dot above a letter means write down that letter, and an arrow means write down either the previous letter or the next one.

Look at the letter on the right. Can you help Abi reveal the hidden message and discover the whereabouts of her aunt?

Dear Margaret,

Let me begin
by offering you my heartfelt thanks
and by saying how we all ate lovely
meals yesterday lunch. Even
my mother and father and my brother
Nathan said that. We have no
knowledge of dear Charles yet
but he is going to send us emails
as soon as the national trials
start on Wednesday. I hope Nick
and Phillip achieve their aims.

Best wishes
Cousin Anna

34

Rail code

The code on these pages is called the rail code because it is said to look like the two rails of a train track.

To write a message in rail code, the first two letters are written one above the other. So, 'Agent Jones nearby' starts: A
                                                     G

Every pair of letters in the message is written out one above the other, until the message is written in two lines, like the parallel lines of a train track:

AETOENAB
GNJNSERY

To make the code harder to crack, the two lines of letters are written next to each other:

AETOENAB GNJNSERY

Here are some secret messages that have been coded using the rail code. Can you work them out?

1. **MEUDRHSAINLCMDIH ETNETETTOCOKINGT**

2. **IILENHTEVTNODNOAI WLBOTEWLEELNOTPRS**

35

Secret sequences

This is like the number jumble code (code 15), where numbers in different sequences stand for letters.

See if you can decode these messages. To help you discover each code's number sequence, part of each message has been decoded for you:

1. 7 19 22 9 22 26 9 22 22 13 22 14 2 8
   T H E R E A

   11 18 22 8 18 13 7 19 22 26 9 22 26.

A	B	C	D	E	F	G	H	I	J	K	L	M

N	O	P	Q	R	S	T	U	V	W	X	Y	Z

2. 14 18 4 14 24 30 24 16 44 14 38 44 52 40
   T R Y T O L O S

   44 26 14 14 18 52 36 30 36 26 40 4 24 12.

A	B	C	D	E	F	G	H	I	J	K	L	M

N	O	P	Q	R	S	T	U	V	W	X	Y	Z

3. 13 37 43 27 43 43 13 35 25 39 7
   T H E M E E

35 29 29 49 43 37 43 29 45 51 13

27 35 45 45 51 3 23 25 41 17.

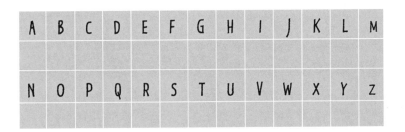

4. 9 45 39 15 60 45 60 24 15 9 45
   C O M E T

18 18 15 15 57 24 45 42 39 3 27

42 57 60 54 15 15 60.

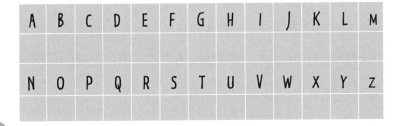

36

Secrets at sea

Jake is on a cruise with his family. One afternoon, he decides to spend some time by himself, exploring the ship. After a while, he comes across a series of dark, deserted cabins and notices strange symbols on the walls. Some of the symbols have letters written below them – as if they are a code. Is it a secret message?

Look at the symbols on the right. Can you help Jake discover what the message says from the symbols that have already been decoded? Write the message under the symbols.

STOLEN

THE

I

ARE

PLEASE

37

Dummy code no. 2

This code is a variation of the dummy code (code 13). A message is divided into even-numbered groups of letters and a 'dummy' letter is put in the middle, as for the dummy code. For example, 'They have used the dummy code' becomes:

THTEY HAIVE USPED THOED UMGMY COBDE

Then, each group of letters is written back-to-front:

YETHT EVIAH DEPSU DEOHT YMGMU EDBOC

See if you can understand these coded messages:

1. ONXOD EELMT EGFAT LBMTN HSEEU LIIWE

VIYGL UOFYE SLOAF FNPIE AMCRO NOOIT.

2. ONGGI RPLER OIXVE EMSSU GALSS KECWE

IWMON ASFIT PAORT.

38

Cryptic board game code

Agent Z is working for a top-secret, crime-fighting detective agency. One of his fellow agents has been kidnapped and Agent Z has information that he is being held in a deserted mansion on the outskirts of the city. When he reaches the mansion, the only thing he can find is an old board and some mysterious-looking tiles. Might this give some clues as to the whereabouts of the agent? Can you help Agent Z solve the puzzle?

Match the pieces on the left to the board, and cross off the squares as you find them. When you have done this, only a few squares will remain uncovered. These will spell out a secret message.

39

Mixed-up menu

The
Fine Diner

1 Mashed parsnip
2 Vegetable delight
3 Omelette

4 Meatball ice cream
5 Garlic snails
6 Beef in custard
7 Haddock cheesecake
8 Cheese pizza
9 Teriyaki turnip

10 Steamed cockles
11 Chocolate chip cabbage
12 Roast mackerel
13 Hot pork pudding

Secret Agent Alex is at a restaurant, celebrating his brother's birthday. The waiter hands him a menu, but the choice of dishes seems strange. It looks like the menu might be hiding a secret message. See if you can help Alex by reading the menu on the left and finding the secret message. (Hint: look at code 9 for clues.)

As Alex is puzzling over this message, he notices another one scribbled on his napkin. Look at code 17 and help Alex decode the message below.

RNETSHCEUSETMOERIEACMULPOBCOKAERDDI

BCEHWEAFRHEETIHSEAHSEPAYD

40

Postcard from New Zealand

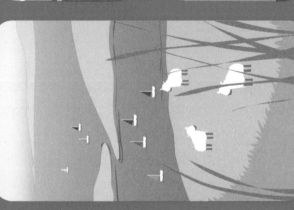

There is a hidden message on this postcard. Can you work out what it says?

Write the message here:

_____

_____

_____

_____

_____

Dear KirsTy,

We are Having a lovEly time in new
ZEaland. we are so PleASed we
came here. sun is alWays shining.
The fOod is wondeRful. do come
and vISit us when you have some
free time. I Know i never Want to
leave!

All our love,

MirIam and Derek.

A B C D E F G H I J K L M N O P Q R S T U V W X Y Z

41

The secret of the star map

Agent Amy has been carrying out close surveillance of the Molonga observatory for two months, ever since she received a tip-off that it is being used as a cover for criminal activities. So far, the only information she has collected from the observatory is maps of stars in the night sky.

As an experienced agent, Amy knows that secret messages can be hidden in the most unexpected places. So, she decides to study these maps more closely. Maybe they hold some clues as to what exactly is going on in the observatory.

One of the maps is shown on the right. Can you help Agent Amy discover its secret? There is something along the edge of an earlier page in this book that will help you uncover a hidden message. Clue: turn the book so the map is at the top, then start at the top and work your way down...

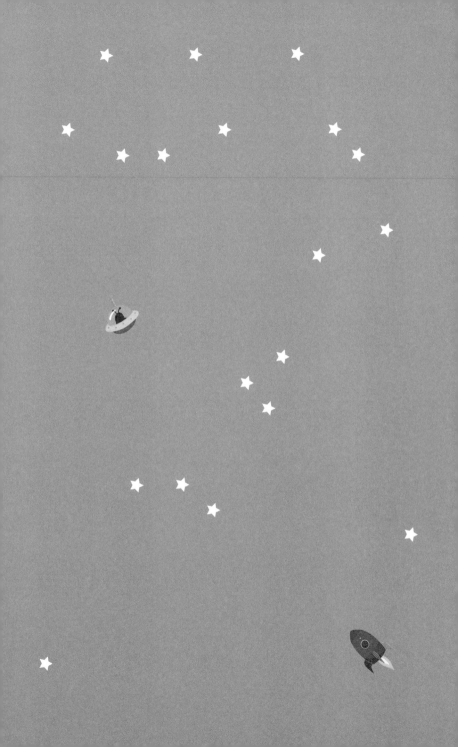

42

Twisty teasers

This teasing code is similar to the looping lines code (code 21), but for this code the loopy pattern changes each time. The message is written out in lines of four, then any pattern can be drawn over the letters:

The coded message is written following the pattern:

PGCS WHSA RIBI TANK

or,   SWIT ABHC GSIN KRAP

or,   TIWS CHBA NISG PARK

Figure out which patterns are used below and crack the codes:

1. **NYMF AOIB ASNK EEIG.**

2. **LLOC ECTN PSWE APER.**

3. **MESS OEGA NPAG OWTE.**

Detective Dean is monitoring a gang called the Crazy Coders who communicate in code. His job is to decode any messages sent between gang members. He has found a phone that belonged to one of the Coders. When he tries to read the text messages he realizes they are in code. Can you help Detective Dean by decoding the messages on the left?

1.

2.

3.

These messages use a different code. Can you help Dean by decoding these, too? Look at code 16 for clues...

1. DIHE YMOEN NI DRE ABG.

2. ALEEV GAB TA TRUARSENAT.

3. I LIWL LOCCLET TI TA YIMDAD.

44

No. 1 Agency:
Top-secret mission

Agent Smith is working for the No. 1 Agency, an organization dedicated to solving mysteries.

He is on a top-secret mission to monitor a factory in the Lostokov forest that is suspected of being a criminal hide-out. At a rendezvous, he finds a document containing the mysterious symbols below. Can you help Agent Smith decode the symbols? Clue: this code has been used before on another No. 1 Agency mission in this book.

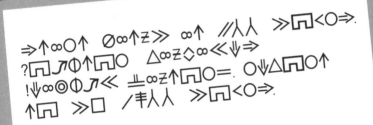

45

Gomoto's unexpected mystery

Eli has spent the last year with the native people of Gomoto. On his final day in their village, he comes across a piece of paper with some symbols written on it. At first, he thinks it's from one of the Gomoto. However, after studying it more closely, he soon discovers that the symbols are not like the Gomoto's language at all. It looks more like a secret code. Can you help Eli by decoding the message below? Look at the opposite page for clues...

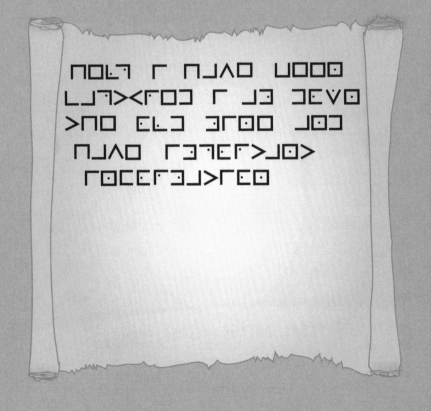

46

Column code

Coding a message in column code is quick and easy, but decoding one will take a little longer.

The first word of a message is written out, then the rest is written below in rows of the same length. (In this example, the rows are seven letters long.) Fill any spaces with an 'X'.

PREPARE
YOURSEL
FFORMIS
SIONXXX

Then, each column of letters is written out from top to bottom, like this:

PYFS ROFI EUOO PRRN ASMX REIX ELSX

Can you understand the message below and the ones on the opposite page? They have all been disguised using the column code.

1. TTAGAT AHCEGR KEKTEE EPAOND.

2. BIYHLY RSWHOX OAAISX WSTMEX NPCCLX.

3. CATEKC AGXAEE LEUFAN LNSACT.

4. DYUNN IOSGD SUIBH GRNEA USGAT IEARX SLLDX EFOAX.

47

Coded combination

Detective Sharp is on the trail of a notorious gang of thieves. They've just pulled off their biggest job yet, stealing some priceless jewels.

Sharp suspects the gang's leader has stashed the jewels in a nearby warehouse. When he gets inside, it's deserted except for a scrap of paper covered in what looks like gibberish, and a huge safe in one corner. Surely the jewels must be inside? Can you help the detective find the safe's combination and defeat the gang's plan?

Well done, boys! We're almost there, but watch out because there's a detective on our trail. I'll try to put him off the scent. Meet me at the West Docks tomorrow as planned. Bring the jewels. The combination for the safe is twenty-five, seventy, zero, forty, eighty-one, zero. The last number is a quarter of what the rest of the combination adds up to. This time tomorrow, we'll be rich!

Decipher the gang leader's coded instructions and write the combination for the safe below. Write down the gang's intended meeting place, too, so they can be caught.

Combination:

Meeting place:

48

Bacon's code

Francis Bacon was an English philosopher and scientist who invented his own way of sending messages in code using bold letters and normal letters. Each group of five letters in the text represented one letter of the secret message, depending on which letters in that group were written normally or in bold. The recipient could split the text into groups of five letters and decipher the real message using the key below. For example, 'We **went to** the **play today**' becomes:

WE**WEN TTOTH E**PLAY **TODAY**

which means: H   E   L   P

A = *****

B = ****B

C = ***B*

D = ***BB

E = **B**

F = **B*B

G = **BB*

H = **BBB

I = *B***

J = *B**B

K = *B*B*

L = *B*BB

M = *BB**

N = *BB*B

O = *BBB*

P = *BBBB

Q = B****

R = B***B

S = B**B*

T = B**BB

U = B*B**

V = B*B*B

W = B*BB*

X = B*BBB

Y = BB***

Z = BB**B

Key:

* = normal

B = bold

Using the key on the left, can you decode the message hidden in this ghostly opening?

The old oak tree swayed and lurched in the high wind, and its branches clawed at the windowpanes like skeletal fingers. Dark, inky storm clouds filled the sky, and the rain fell like tears. Inside, the dogs howled at flashes of lightning that lit the sky and silhouetted the tree for a terrifying instant. Then, right on the stroke of midnight, there came a knock at the door, and all was suddenly calm.

49

Playing-card code

Sophie Cipher is a spy for an elite agency called The Black Suits. One of the ways the agency delivers simple mission instructions is by using a playing-card code. But, in keeping with their name, they only use clubs and spades.

The code uses clubs for the first half of the alphabet, counting **up** from Ace to King (Ace = A, 2 = B, and so on). Then spades are used for the second half of the alphabet, counting **down** from King to Ace (King = N, Queen = O, and so on).

Sophie has just received a small package of playing cards. Being careful not to rearrange them, she splits them into the two fans shown on the right. Reading the top fan from left to right and then the bottom one, can you decode her mission instructions and write them below?

Message:

50

Secret stamp code

Rob is visiting an old aunt who used to be a spy. When he arrives, her house is deserted, but he finds two stamped envelopes at her desk with just one-line addresses on them. On both of them, his aunt has circled the house number, and written a short message. It sounds like she might still be a spy...

He looks around a bit more and finds the piece of paper below. It looks like someone is using the stamps and the house numbers to send coded messages, but the key isn't complete. Next to it is a third, untranslated envelope. Can you help Rob finish filling in the key and work out what the last message says?

B = Blue   Y = Yellow   R = Red

Number	Stamp	Translation
1	R	The target
1	B	Your contact
1		Enemy agent
2		Will arrive by first plane
2		Is going into hiding
2		Is under suspicion
3		Capture immediately
3		Follow and report to HQ
3		Meet on arrival

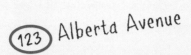

123 Alberta Avenue

Your contact will arrive by first plane. Meet on arrival.

321 Alberta Avenue

Your contact is under suspicion. Follow and report to HQ.

231 Alberta Avenue

51

Twice-coded castle

As an archaeologist, Professor Walls is used to deciphering codes. On a trip to the castle of a medieval king who was famous for his hatred of visitors and his cruel sense of humour, he sees the old banner on the right.

The professor studies it for a few minutes before chuckling to himself. Can you decode the message and see what made the professor laugh? The first numbers have already been decoded. Look at code 16 and code 35 for clues.

A B C D E F G H I J K L M
       22   19
N O P Q R S T U V W X Y Z
              7

22 7 19   8 4 26 11 23 9 12 8
E T H

12 7   22 20 7   12 13 18 7

19 22 7   8 15 22 24 26 7

8 18   13 18 13 9 22 23.

26 4 25 22 26 9   22 19 7

12 20 8 23.   6 2 12   22 5 19 26

22 13 25 22   13 22 9 4 26 23.

52

Missing archaeologist

Anna is staying in a hotel in Cairo, on her way to see her famous uncle. He is an archaeologist, convinced of the existence of a vast amount of gold hidden at the site of the pyramids.

One morning at breakfast, she is handed the local paper and is shocked by a cover story about her uncle. But when she tries to find the rest of the article, there's nothing there except a torn slip of paper with a list of numbers on it.

She begins to suspect that it might be one of her uncle's secret messages, meant for her. Can you help Anna decode the message hidden in the story on the right?

1, 2, 1
1, 3, 2
1, 4, 3
1, 5, 4
1, 5, 6

1, 6, 1
1, 7, 1
1, 7, 6
2, 1, 1
2, 1, 2

2, 3, 1
2, 4, 1
2, 7, 1
2, 7, 3
2, 8, 3

Clue: the numbers direct you to certain words on the page. The first number is the column number, the second is the line number, and the third is the word number.

ay there
amazing
eclipse
Egypt
Moon
years
ee an
rowd
own
eet.
ody
to
an
ht
d
l

Famous archaeologist goes missing

Professor Spades, famous for the discovery of Cleopatra's lost obelisk and a host of other high profile projects, is missing in the field – a sad shadow over his years of great work.

The latest dig, set to entrance the world once more, was halted when he went missing at dusk three days ago while out on an evening stroll.

"I don't know what could have happened," said the local police chief, "but we shall not rest until we have found out – the professor is a rare international treasure."

continued on page 7

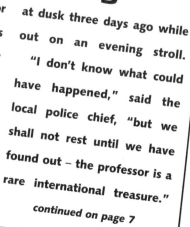

r
s
W
go
zo
by

Scribbling space

You can use this page if you need more space to decipher the hidden messages in some of the codes.

Answers

1 Meet agent 9 at the old market to pick up your disguise.
She will have a red rose.

2 1. Always act in a way that looks normal. Do not attract
unnecessary attention. 2. Wear clothes that make you blend in
with your surroundings and the people around you. 3. Carry a
newspaper or large handkerchief so that you can quickly
hide your face. 4. Hide behind things, like trees, whenever you
can. 5. If you think you have been spotted, quickly change
your disguise.

3 Meet me at 1400 hours. I've got the gems.

4 Dear Arthur, Congratulations on your escape. I have heard
you need help to catch the people who kidnapped you. I will
leave a brown package on the park bench near the marble
statue. Wednesday. Nine pm. Signed RF.

5 1. Here lies King Kamun. He who reads this will find great
riches. The treasure is hidden under my statue. Beware the
curse. 2. I have already taken the treasure. You are too late!

6 1. crash-proof motor-powered snowmobile.
2. frost-resistant radio. 3. snow-vision goggles.
4. polar bear repellent. 5. portable microwave.

7 1. Ambush enemy agents tomorrow night.
2. Agent Red go undercover.

8 We must meet at nine outside the old house. I have the money.
The gold from the last job is hidden under the stairs.

Answers

9 1. Meet me at seven. 2. Code name banana.

10 1. Leave a false trail/Footprint. 2. Speak with an accent/
Change voice. 3. Give a different name/Confuse.

11 1. (Q=A, R=B... P=Z) What game do secret agents play? I-spy!
2. (T=A, U=B... S=Z) What do you cook for a secret agent?
Spy-ghetti!

12 1. Poisoned umbrella. 2. Spy vision goggles. 3. Magnifying glass.

13 1. All the money found last night is fake. Report to Q.
2. The real money was sent overseas yesterday.
3. Monitor all known spy gangs in local area.

14 1. Watch for agent 19. 2. Wait for further instructions Agent
Smith. 3. To signal for help raise your right hand.
4. Code red. Agent get out now! 5. AWT HCF ROW MOA CNA RRY
NIG ERD ABG. 6. GAE TNY LEL WOY UOA ERB IEN FGO LLO EWD.
7. ERT RUN OTA EGN YCH AED FOF CIE. 8. EME ITN IGS TAS VEE DNO
ONT EBL TAE.

15 1. Contact HQ immediately. (A=1, B=2, C=3, D=4... Z=26)
2. Warning. You are being followed. (A=2, B=4, C=6... Z=52)
3. Watch Smith closely. She is a spy. (A=1, B=3, C=5... Z=51)

16 1. Fake beard and a wig. 2. Hat and dark glasses.
3. Walk with a limp. 4. Black eye and sling.

17 1. The water is poisoned. Do not drink.
2. Meet in park. Will be by the hot dog stand.
3. Instructions in locker 14.

Answers

18 Attention Agent White. Change disguise.

19 Use the device along the edge of the previous page. Turn the book so the postcard is at the top, then slowly slide the device down over the map from the top. When a red dot on the map meets a letter on the device, write it down. It will spell out the message: Agent return to base.

20 1. Follow woman in hat. 2. Put on disguise.

21 1. Turn left by river. 2. Meet at crossroads. 3. Directions in cabinet room 36.

22 1. The keyword for message two is DECOYS. 2. The keyword for message three is NIGHT. 3. Well done! You have cracked all the codes!

23 The message has been coded using the cross code. It says: Leave the train four stops from the end.
The poster's message has been coded using the hidden word code. It says: Help. Tell HQ Agent Y is missing.

24 City Museum, October 19th, between 8:30pm and 8:40pm, Egyptian jewels.

25 1. The HQ of any spy agency is called Uncle.
2. A double agent is a spy that works for two countries at the same time.
3. A dead drop is a secret place where spies leave packages or messages to be picked up.

26 1. The password is red fox. 2. Follow Agent Black now.
3. Package at dead drop.

Answers

27 Here are the words with missing letters – **Across:** feather, land, wait, her, lava, we, tables, key, expand, spiked. **Down:** tapping, ladle, data, waded, even, hot, any, shield, redden, newt, ask. The message reads: Help I have been kidnapped.

28 1. Man overboard. 2. Fire in the hold. 3. Ahoy there.

29 Time: midnight tonight. Intended target: Fingers McCoy. Names of criminals involved: Big Bad Bob, Sandy the Snitch and Dangerous Dave.

30 Meet me in the usual place. I have the money. Do not be late.

31 1. This is Bad Bruno. Operation Big Money is in place. Send signal to gang members now. 2. This is Terrible Tyson. Signal sent. All set for Friday. City Bank. Twelve noon. 3. This is Bad Bruno. Cover your tracks carefully. I think we are being watched.

32 The label has been disguised using the decoy code. It says: Mr. Willis, London, England. (Agent X is the decoy phrase.)
The message inside has been coded using puzzling numbers. It says: Please help. I am in the hands of enemy spies. Tell HQ.

33 A dot above a letter means that letter, this symbol '<' means the previous letter, and this symbol '>' means the next letter. The message reads: Leave now destination China.

34 1. Meet under the station clock. Midnight.
2. I will be on the twelve ten, London to Paris.

35 1. There are enemy spies in the area. (A=26, B=25... Z=1)
2. Agent Z is a double agent. (Z=1, Y=3, X=5... A=51)
3. Try to lose the agent trailing you. (Z=2, Y=4, X=6... A=52)

Answers

36 Stolen treasure is hidden on the ship. I know where it is and who the thieves are. I was kidnapped before I could tell the captain. Please rescue me.

37 1. Do not meet Agent Blue. She will give you false information.
2. Ignore previous message. We know it is a trap.

38 In the cellar.

39 This is a variation of the shopping list code. Look at the numbers by the different dishes and write down the corresponding letters. The message reads: Meet in kitchen. The second message has been coded using the sandwich code. It says: Rescue me. I am locked in the store cupboard. Beware the head chef. He is a spy.

40 The new password is kiwi. (Look out for lower case and capital letters in the wrong places.)

41 Use the device along the edge of the previous page. Turn the book so the map is at the top, then slide the device down over the map. Whenever a star meets a letter on the device, write down that letter. It will spell out: The diamonds are ready.

42 1. Fake money is in bag. 2. Collect newspaper.
3. Message on page two.

43 1. Next job is Monday three pm. 2. Jewel shop. High Street. Bring black clothing. 3. Watch your backs. Detective spotted nearby. The next three messages have been disguised using the anagram code. 1. Hide money in red bag. 2. Leave bag at restaurant. 3. I will collect it at midday.

Answers

44 Look at code number 1 and use this to figure out what the symbols stand for. The message says: Start watch at 11:00 hours. Monitor packages leaving factory. Report to HQ 12:00 hours.

45 Help I have been captured. I am down the old mine and have important information.

46 1. Take the package to Agent Red. 2. Brown is a spy. Watch him closely. 3. Call Agent X. Use a fake accent. 4. Disguise yourself using a long beard and hat.

47 The combination is: 25, 70, 0, 40, 81, 0, 54. The meeting place is the West Docks.

48 I have important information about a double agent. Meet me at the old shipyard.

49 Submarine. Dock six. Monday.

50 Enemy agent is going into hiding. Capture immediately.

51 The password to get into the castle is dinner. Beware of the dogs. You have been warned.

52 The obelisk projects a shadow over the entrance at dusk. I have found the treasure.